Spiritual Sparks

A READER

Spiritual Sparks

A READER

REFLECTIONS ON MEANING, PURPOSE,
AND THE SPIRITUAL DIMENSION OF EVERYDAY LIFE

BY ZE'EV SMASON

SPIRITUAL SPARKS: A READER

Published by Spiritual Sparks Publishing, LLC
St. Louis, Missouri

ISBN (paperback): 979-8-9959795-0-0
ISBN (hardcover): 979-8-9959795-1-7

First Edition

Cover design by Naosha Pere
Typesetting by Mark Karis
Proofreading by Sean Strain

Printed in the United States of America

TO CHANI —

For all that is mine is yours.

WITH GRATITUDE

Those who helped bring this book to light

FOUNDING CIRCLE

Stephen and Sandy Bell
Don and Julie Eisenberg
Jan Hardcastle
Faye Cohen McCary and Brian McCary
Dr. Irvin Pretsky
Arin Rosenberg
Doug and Margy Weisman

PATRONS

Eldad and Danielle Bialecki
The Feigenbaum-Pepose Family
Janet and Alan Haber
Jay and Peggy Umansky
Bruce and Faith Waxman
Anonymous

SUPPORTERS

Larry and Faith Comensky
Stanley and Rhonnie Goldfader
Sandy Greenberg
Cantor Murray and Joyce Hochberg
Sheryl Levine
Joan and Don Weis

CONTENTS

OPENING REFLECTION

We all sense that there's a difference between ***living*** *and being* ***truly alive****.*

Life can be full of responsibilities and routines, yet something essential can still feel just out of reach.

And then there are times when that changes.

A conversation that lingers.

A moment of clarity.

A feeling of connection to another person, to the world, perhaps even to something beyond ourselves.

Or a moment when we step beyond ourselves and give.

A word, an action, a kindness.

Something offered to another.

In those moments, life feels present.

We recognize those moments immediately.

The question is… why don't they last?

INTRODUCTION

A Reader's Guide to *Spiritual Sparks*

We live in a world filled with noise. Information is everywhere, and distraction is always close. Yet beneath all the activity of daily life, most people still carry **an inner longing**: to live with more meaning, more clarity, and more inner depth.

That longing is not a weakness. It is not escapism. It is something noble. It is the soul's way of reminding us that we were created for more than survival, more than busyness, and more than comfort.

Spiritual Sparks: A Reader is a collection of sixteen essays, organized into four sections, each one exploring a different dimension of the inner life. These essays are not meant to overwhelm you with information or demand that you adopt a particular religious framework. They are meant to offer a different kind of experience: a moment of reflection, a shift in perspective, and a gentle invitation to live more awake.

Each essay follows a simple structure. It begins with a story or idea that opens the theme. It then offers three core insights to help deepen understanding and bring the message into daily life. Finally, it closes with two quotes and a question, not as a test, but as a way of helping the ideas remain with you after the page is turned.

You do not need to read this book in order. You can begin anywhere. You can read one essay slowly, revisit it later, and allow its message to unfold over time. Some essays may speak to you immediately. Others may become meaningful only when life brings you to the place where you need them.

The first section, **Inner Essence**, explores the foundational truth that each person carries a spiritual core, an inner self that longs for meaning, goodness, and purpose. The second section, **Inner Life**, explores qualities that shape our emotional and spiritual resilience, awe, peace of mind, hope, and the ability to respond when life hurts. The third section, **Relationships**, turns outward, exploring empathy, love, friendship, and forgiveness, the qualities that make human connection not only possible, but deeply transformative. The final section, **Life in the World**, focuses on how spirituality expresses itself through how we see the world and how we contribute to it, through beauty, gratitude, excellence, and the responsibility to become a light to others.

The goal of this reader is not perfection. It is movement. Not dramatic transformation overnight, but steady spiritual growth, one insight, one question, one choice at a time.

If even one essay helps you live with more meaning, more warmth, or more clarity, then it has done what it was meant to do.

RABBI ZE'EV SMASON

SECTION I

Inner Essence

Before we try to improve our lives, we have to remember what we are.

Beneath personality, achievement, and even mood, there is something steady and real within us.

Call it the soul, the self, the inner spark, or simply the "you beneath it all."

This first section is about returning to that core. Not as an abstract idea, but as a lived experience.

Because when we forget our essence, we live shallowly, reactively, and anxiously.

And when we remember it, we gain self-knowledge, purpose, and direction.

ESSAY #1

What Is Spirituality?

NURTURING YOUR INNER ESSENCE

We yearn for a spiritually vibrant life, yet often struggle to know how to reach it.

What do we really mean when we talk about spirituality? It's a word often used to evoke comfort or inspiration, yet its true depth can be overlooked. Spirituality is more than a feel-good slogan. It is a deeper dimension that gives our lives meaning, direction, and purpose. To understand spirituality, we first need to understand what makes us uniquely human.

WHAT MAKES US HUMAN: BEYOND SUPER-INTELLIGENT APES

RECOGNIZING THE SPARK BEYOND BIOLOGY

Science calls us *Homo sapiens*, "wise humans." We share many traits with animals. They can crack coconuts; we can launch satellites. But if the difference is only brainpower, then perhaps we're simply apes running upgraded software.

Yet almost everyone senses there's something more.

Spirituality begins with a simple truth: we are not merely clever animals. We are souls, infused with an inner spark that reaches beyond biology. That inner life—that part of us that searches, questions, and aspires—is the essence of spirituality.

THE THREE UNIQUE CAPACITIES OF THE SOUL

HUNGER FOR MEANING, PURPOSE, AND VIRTUE

Our soul expresses itself in three distinctive capacities:

- **The hunger for meaning:** asking, "Why am I here?"
- **The drive for purpose:** choosing growth over passing pleasure
- **The call to virtue:** choosing what is right over what is easy

These capacities shape how we listen, how we love, and how we decide what matters most.

CREATING A SPIRITUALLY VIBRANT LIFE

GROWING SPIRITUAL DEPTH THROUGH CHOICE

A spiritually vibrant life begins with seeking meaning, asking the great existential question, "What's it all about?" and searching for real answers.

We pursue purpose through decisions that foster growth and change. Unlike animals, we ponder legacy and wrestle with moral dilemmas. That searching is part of the gift of being human.

And we choose virtue over vice by exercising free will. In the end, our spiritual identity is shaped less by what we feel, and more by the choices we make.

This truth echoes in two very different voices:

> *"God formed the human from the dust of the earth, and He blew into his nostrils the breath of life ..."*
>
> —GENESIS 2:7

> *"We are not human beings having a spiritual experience. We are spiritual beings having a human experience."*
>
> —PIERRE TEILHARD DE CHARDIN

A QUESTION TO CARRY WITH YOU

Where in your everyday life do you feel spiritually alive?

Perhaps in a moment of choosing patience over frustration, helping someone without recognition, or pausing to appreciate the beauty around you.

You don't need a dramatic answer. Even noticing those moments is already a form of spiritual awakening.

A spiritually rich life doesn't require a mountaintop retreat or sudden reinvention. It begins with quiet introspection: *Am I living with meaning? Where am I going? Can I release some of the distractions that fill my days?* Each question opens the door to deeper connection with your truest self.

ESSAY #2

The Soul Is Your Essence

THE "YOU" INSIDE YOU

There is a part of you that remains steady through every season of life.

It exists beneath shifting moods and changing circumstances, beyond successes and failures, and even deeper than the body that carries you through the world. You may not think about it often, but you sense it when something rings deeply true, when beauty moves you, or when acting against your better nature leaves you unsettled.

That enduring inner presence is not a role you play or a personality you've developed. It is the animating center of who you are—the source of your deepest longings, your moral awareness, and your search for meaning. It is who you are at your core.

YOU DON'T HAVE A SOUL. YOU ARE A SOUL

THE DEEPER SELF BENEATH EVERY ROLE

Many people define themselves by their body—by their reflection in the mirror, or how others perceive them. Others turn inward, identifying with their thoughts or even with their personality. But your soul isn't any of these. It is the deeper "you," the self beneath all expression. Classic wisdom teaches that we are a synthesis of body and soul, physical and spiritual. The body walks us through the world … but the soul is who we are.

SOME TRUTHS RESONATE BECAUSE THEY'VE ALWAYS BEEN PART OF US

WHY MORALITY FEELS INNATE

Have you ever just known that something was right or wrong without knowing how?

Before we learn words, something within us recognizes what is virtuous and ethical. A Yale study found that babies, even months old, instinctively favor helpfulness and recoil from harm. Long before language or instruction, they reveal an inner moral compass.

We don't begin life as a blank slate, a *tabula rasa*. These truths aren't learned from scratch; they're embedded within us, recognized and carried by the soul.

THE SOUL LONGS FOR MEANING MORE THAN COMFORT

PURPOSE NOURISHES WHAT PHYSICALITY CANNOT

Some of the most meaningful work in the world—caregiving, special education, nursing—often comes with modest pay. And yet, people choose these paths. Many volunteer time and resources, forgoing comfort and momentary pleasure. Why?

Selflessness emerges from the soul, which is drawn toward meaning. At the deepest level, we recognize that a life devoted only to ease feels empty, while a life oriented toward giving feels whole.

The world contains two kinds of people: givers and takers. Our soul yearns to give. Comfort may soothe the body, but the soul is nourished by purpose.

This truth echoes in two very different voices:

"The soul is always praying—even when the lips are still."

—RABBI ABRAHAM ISAAC KOOK

"It's all about soul. It's all about knowing what someone is feeling."

—BILLY JOEL, "ALL ABOUT SOUL"

A QUESTION TO CARRY WITH YOU

What's a moment when you knew your soul was leading—not your body, not your ego, but something deeper?

Often, the soul doesn't shout. It simply nudges us toward what is truer, kinder, and more lasting.

Whatever moment comes to mind, hold onto it. It's a reminder that the deepest part of you already knows the way.

May you be guided not by what the mirror shows, but by what your soul already knows.

May your days be shaped by light, insight, and a deeper connection to who you truly are—your soul

ESSAY #3

A Good Heart: The Jewel Within

WHERE HUMANITY MEETS SPIRITUALITY

Famed actor and comedian Alan Alda met the love of his life over a ruined rum cake.

In 1956, at a mutual friend's dinner party, Alda was introduced to Arlene Weiss. During the evening, the hostess accidentally dropped a rum cake onto the kitchen floor. Mortified, the guests looked on in awkward silence. All but two, that is. Alda and Weiss quietly took spoons and began eating the cake, not out of hunger, but out of kindness, unwilling to let the hostess feel embarrassed.

That small, spontaneous act marked the beginning of a lifelong partnership. The couple married a year later and recently celebrated their sixty-eighth wedding anniversary.

What moved them to act so instinctively? No rule book guided them. No calculation intervened. Before thought could interfere, something within them recognized what the moment required. Classic wisdom teaches that a good heart lies at the very center of a vibrant spiritual life.

THE POWER OF A GOOD HEART

THE QUALITY THAT CARRIES ALL OTHER QUALITIES

A good heart is more than kindness. It is a spiritual superpower. Just as the physical heart pumps life-giving blood to every organ of the body, a good heart circulates virtue through every part of our being.

A good heart already contains the seeds of every other quality, simply waiting to be expressed. Patience, humility, integrity, and compassion are not forced into existence. They emerge naturally, in their own time.

Classic wisdom teaches that this is the greatest quality we can cultivate, for it becomes the wellspring from which all other spiritual strengths flow.

THE TWO HEARTS WITHIN

CHOOSING THE HEART THAT LEADS UPWARD

Each of us lives with two hearts: one that uplifts, and one that distracts.

Inside us exists a tug-of-war: one heart seeks meaning, truth, and what endures; the other seeks comfort, ease, and the passing moment.

Which heart will we follow, the one of soul, or the one of self?

The good heart is drawn to love, to reaching our potential, to that which nourishes the soul. To stay attentive to that inner voice, we sometimes need to remind ourselves of a simple intention: *I want to be good.* Held gently in awareness, that intention begins to shape our choices and illuminate our path.

SOFTENING THE HEART

HOW LIFE OPENS WHAT WAS CLOSED

Classic sources teach that the heart is like an unplowed field: naturally hard and resistant, unable to receive nourishment until the soil is softened through cultivation. Our hearts, too, must be opened, and this happens through both joy and sorrow.

Joy waters the heart through gratitude. Difficulty opens it through empathy.

The invitation is to let both do their softening work. When we allow life's experiences to touch us deeply, and open our hearts to others, we nurture our own soul. That is where vibrant spirituality comes alive.

This truth echoes in two very different voices:

> *"Keep your heart with all vigilance, for from it flow the springs of life."*
>
> —PROVERBS 4:23

> *"A good heart is the best religion; its light is the most powerful light."*
>
> —MEHMET MURAT İLDAN

A QUESTION TO CARRY WITH YOU

What's one challenge you face in choosing truth and meaning over ease and comfort?

Whatever comes to mind, notice it without judgment. The very fact that you care is a sign that your good heart is already awake.

Neil Young's 1972 classic *Heart of Gold* captures a universal spiritual longing: "I want to live, I want to give. I've been a miner for a heart of gold." We're all miners, searching for sincerity and depth of connection, not only with others, but within our own soul.

The good news is that the heart of gold isn't buried somewhere far away. It is the jewel within you, waiting to be polished by awareness, opened through experience, and awakened by intention.

May you discover and nurture your heart of gold.

ESSAY #4

Purpose: Why Am I Here?

THE DOORWAY TO A PURPOSEFUL LIFE

A palliative care nurse who spent years speaking with people in their final days once shared a striking observation. When the noise of life fell away and clarity set in, many people voiced the same regret. Of all the regrets she heard, one surfaced more than any other.

"I wish I'd had the courage to live a life true to myself," they said, "not the life others expected of me."

This was the most common regret she encountered, later

included in her book *The Top Five Regrets of the Dying*. When people look back, they don't wish they had done more. They wish they had been more faithful to who they truly were.

That realization leads to one of life's deepest questions: *Why am I here?* Not in the sense of achievement or accomplishment, but in the deeper sense of purpose. Purpose, in this sense, is not something we invent. It is something we uncover.

THE HUMAN CAPACITY TO SEEK PURPOSE

THE SOUL AWAKENS THROUGH THE QUESTION

We are wired to ask: *Why am I here? What is my purpose? What is the meaning of my existence?*

The ache for meaning is one of the most basic expressions of our spiritual essence. A giraffe munching on leaves never pauses to ask, "Is this what life is all about?"

To seek purpose is to acknowledge that life is more than survival or success. Actualizing our spirituality begins not with certainty, but with the willingness to search. The very act of asking awakens the soul, stirring our deepest essence to seek.

THE UNIQUENESS OF EACH PERSON'S MISSION

YOU WEREN'T MADE TO BE SOMEONE ELSE

You weren't made to be Moses, da Vinci, or Michael Jordan. The divine question isn't, "Why weren't you them?" but, "Why didn't you become you?"

Your mission is as unique as your fingerprint, and just as intentional. The stars are named. You were named in love, to share love.

You are one of a kind, with a mission that can shift with each season of your life, never lived before—and never to be repeated.

THE GATEWAY TO PURPOSE: SELF-KNOWLEDGE AND ACTION

LIVING OUTWARD BEGINS WITH KNOWING INWARD

The journey inward is the first step toward living outward with purpose.

Woe to the person who doesn't know their faults, for they don't know what to correct. Double woe to the one who doesn't know their strengths, for they are unaware of their gifts.

Purpose doesn't live in thought alone. A ship is safe in a harbor, but ships are made to sail, and so are we.

When you act from who you truly are, you walk with purpose. Action, in this sense, is not about doing more, but about expressing more faithfully who you already are.

The soul doesn't seek perfection. It seeks participation.

This truth echoes in two very different voices:

> *"Teach us to number our days, then we shall acquire a heart of wisdom."*
>
> —PSALM 90:12

"Millions long for immortality ... yet don't know what to do on a rainy Sunday afternoon."

—SUSAN ERTZ

A QUESTION TO CARRY WITH YOU

What are your superpowers—the gifts that make you feel most alive and help others come alive too?

Whatever comes to mind, take it seriously. Your gifts are often the clearest clues to why you are here.

Purpose begins within, but it is never meant to remain there. When we know ourselves clearly and act from that place, life gains direction and depth.

From here, the work is not to strive for more, but to live more faithfully, allowing what is within us to shape how we engage the world.

SECTION II

Inner Life

Once we reconnect with who we are, we begin to notice what is happening inside us.

Thoughts, emotions, memories, fears, hopes, and longings … these form the landscape of the inner life.

Most of us move through that landscape quickly, without much awareness.

This section invites you to slow down and listen more carefully.

To recognize what you are feeling, and what those feelings may be trying to teach you.

Inner life is where resilience is formed, where awe breaks through, and where perspective is regained.

It is not a retreat from reality; it is how we gain focus to become the very best version of our potential selves.

ESSAY #5

Awe

WHEN OUR INNER LIFE EXPANDS

In 1965, astronaut Ed White stepped out of his Gemini 4 capsule for America's first spacewalk. As the minutes passed, mission control ordered him to return. White resisted. "I'm not coming in," he said. "This is fun!"

When he finally climbed back inside, he added something unexpected: "It's the saddest moment of my life."

Years later, astronaut Alan Shepard stood on the surface of the moon and looked back at Earth. From that remote distance, our planet appeared fragile, luminous, and alone. Shepard wept.

Scientists now refer to this experience as the overview effect, a shift in perspective that comes from seeing our planet from space. White was overwhelmed by the vastness of the cosmos; Shepard by the beauty and vulnerability of home. Either way, orientation shifts, and something within the observer changes with it.

Most of us will never float in space or stand on the moon. But awe is not reserved for astronauts. It belongs to our soul, waiting not for escape from Earth, but for a way of seeing.

AWE EXPANDS THE INNER LIFE WITHOUT DIMINISHING THE SELF

SMALL, YET NEVER DIMINISHED

Awe is the sense of amazement that arises when we encounter something larger than ourselves, vastness, beauty, or moral depth that cannot be easily explained. It may appear while standing before a sweeping landscape, listening to music that stirs something wordless within us, or witnessing an act of human goodness that feels deeply courageous.

What makes awe distinctive is its paradox. In moments of awe, we feel small, aware of our limits and fragility, and yet we do not feel diminished. Instead, the inner life expands. The self loosens its grip at the center, and something larger comes into view.

Awe restores proportion. It gently shifts attention away from constant self-reference and reminds us that we are part of something broader, deeper, and more meaningful than our immediate concerns. In that moment, without argument or instruction, the inner voice recognizes: *this matters.*

AWE FADES WHEN FAMILIARITY NARROWS THE INNER LENS

WHEN WONDER BECOMES WALLPAPER

Children live with awe. The world feels new, vivid, and endlessly surprising. But over time, familiarity dulls attention. Yesterday's wonder becomes today's wallpaper.

The extraordinary becomes invisible through repetition. A sunrise, the intricate design of a leaf, the birth of a child—what once astonished us slowly recedes into the background. Not because it has lost its beauty, but because our inner lens has narrowed.

As a result, we move through much of life on autopilot. We relate to people as roles, experiences as interruptions, and days as tasks to be completed. When awe fades, life does not collapse. It simply contracts. Depth thins. Meaning feels more distant.

What is lost is not the astounding nature of existence, but our inner openness to it.

AWE RESPONDS TO HOW WE STAND BEFORE LIFE

WONDER IS A POSTURE, NOT A LOCATION

Awe responds to a particular way of meeting the world. When we are attentive and open, awe often appears, not through spectacle, but through what we allow ourselves to notice.

We don't need extraordinary circumstances to encounter it. Awe emerges when we notice the amazement already before us: the elegant spiral of a sunflower, the dignity of a store clerk doing their work well, the raw power of a stormy sky. These moments await our notice.

When we remain receptive, something within us awakens. Awe becomes a gateway to transcendence, not an escape from life or a momentary thrill, but a reminder of depth already present within us. The soul rises when it notices that it is part of something vast, meaningful, and alive.

This truth echoes in two very different voices:

> *"When I behold Your heavens, the work of Your fingers, the moon and the stars that You have set in place . . ."*
>
> —PSALM 8

> *"Two things fill the mind with ever new and increasing admiration and awe: the starry heavens above and the moral law within."*
>
> —IMMANUEL KANT

A QUESTION TO CARRY WITH YOU

What might you be taking for granted today that once filled you with wonder?

Whatever comes to mind, pause for a moment and look again. Awe is often less about discovering something new, and more about recovering what we once knew how to see.

In 1997, Bill Gates spoke to a large audience at a science convention in Seattle. At the time, his personal wealth was estimated at $35 billion. During the question-and-answer period, a physician stood and asked him, "Mr. Gates, if you were blind, would you trade all of your money to have your sight restored?"

Gates did not hesitate. “I’d trade all my money for my sight.”

Awe-inspiring wonders surround us every day. But when familiarity dulls attention, even what is remarkable can fade into the background. Awe begins when we learn to notice again.

ESSAY #6

When Life Hurts

FROM THE WOUND ITSELF COMES THE HEALING

Some of life's deepest lessons don't arrive in moments of clarity and calm. They come through disruption. Through pain. Through moments that leave us reeling, shaking us to the core of our essence.

When life hurts, it interrupts our routines and softens our defenses. The noise of everyday distraction fades, and something deeper begins to speak. Not loudly. Not with answers neatly arranged. But with a message that asks to be listened to rather than solved.

This essay is about finding meaning when life hurts, not by ignoring pain, but by listening for what it signals within us. Because beneath the discomfort, our inner life is stirred to consider how to respond.

PAIN IS A LANGUAGE

WHAT SUFFERING IS TRYING TO SAY

Pain is not only a challenge. It is a message.

Some pain speaks plainly. A toothache doesn't require contemplation. It says: *Pay attention. Something is wrong.* Other forms of hurt are more opaque. Emotional pain, relational strain, disappointment, or loss do not arrive with clear instructions. But they, too, are signals

When pain is only endured, it remains only an experience of suffering. Suffering may intensify if we ignore what pain is trying to tell us, not because pain disappears when we listen, but because unattended pain often deepens and hardens.

This does not mean that every wound can be healed. Some pain remains. Some losses cannot be undone. But even then, pain presents the opportunity to consider a response.

From the wound itself comes the healing, not as a promise of relief, but as the soul's language calling for attention. Pain narrows our focus. It strips away distraction. It raises our inner questions closer to the surface: *What is happening within me? What does this moment ask of me? Can I live with what cannot be changed? If so, how?*

WHEN OUR UNDERSTANDING REACHES ITS LIMITS

WHAT PAIN REVEALS ABOUT OUR ASSUMPTIONS

Pain has a way of showing us where our understanding of life reaches its limits.

We live by assumptions that help life feel navigable: a certain rhythm to our days, a degree of predictability, a sense that effort will be met with proportionate reward. These expectations help us make sense of a complex world and move through it with confidence.

When life hurts, those assumptions are often strained, or shaken. Not because they were faulty, but because they were never meant to carry this much weight. Pain doesn't accuse us of misunderstanding life. It shows us where our understanding may need an added perspective.

This is why pain can feel so disorienting. It unsettles not only what we are experiencing, but how we have been interpreting our lives. Familiar explanations fall silent. Old frameworks offer less comfort. Our inner world, once organized by expectation, feels suddenly exposed and uncertain.

Yet this moment is not a failure of insight. When what once explained life falls short, the inner life is invited to deepen. Not to grasp for answers, but to remain present with questions that now insist on being faced.

Pain does not dismantle meaning. It clears space for a fuller one to emerge, shaped not by certainty, but by attentiveness and depth.

CHOOSING HOW TO LIVE FORWARD

PRESENCE, THEN TRANSFORMATION

When life hurts, a response does not always require action. Often, presence and awareness are the wiser path.

Not every pain can be resolved. Not every loss yields understanding. Experiences may change us without explaining themselves. In those moments, the most meaningful response is not to fix what cannot be fixed, but to consider how we will carry what remains.

This is where the inner life asserts itself. Pain forces questions we would rather avoid:

What do I really value? Who am I becoming through this? Would this pain benefit from a response? And if so, what step would be best?

These questions do not arrive gently, and they do not demand immediate answers. But they signal a shift from endurance alone toward thoughtful engagement.

Researchers have observed that some people, when facing deep disruption, eventually experience what has been called post-traumatic growth, not because pain improves them, but because it prompts a re-examination of priorities, values, and direction. This is simply a possibility that can emerge when pain is met with attention rather than avoidance.

In this sense, spirituality does not bypass suffering. It stays with it. It allows pain to challenge old assumptions and, over time, to reshape how one lives forward. Not through sudden clarity, but through gradual understanding. Through small, deliberate choices: to remain attentive rather than numb, to recognize grief without allowing it to define the whole of one's identity, to live honestly with questions that have not yet found resolution.

Living forward with pain requires presence, not certainty. And over time, that presence may become transformation, not by erasing the wound, but by allowing life to grow around it.

This truth echoes in two very different voices:

"For though the righteous one may fall seven times, he will arise, but the wicked ones will be brought down by adversity."

—PROVERBS 24:16

"Get outside of that box that you've grown accustomed to … Be your own person."

—BO JACKSON

A QUESTION TO CARRY WITH YOU

Has a challenging or painful experience ever become a turning point in your inner life?

Whatever comes to mind, don't rush past it. Sometimes the most important change begins not when the pain disappears, but when we begin to meet it with awareness.

When we hurt, our inner life is not asking to be hurried or resolved. It is asking for attention and presence. Healing does not always mean relief from suffering. Sometimes it means becoming more open, more aware, and more faithful to what life is asking of us now. From the wound itself, something essential may begin to enter.

And in one luminous line, a poet captured it: "The wound is the place where the Light enters you."

—RUMI

ESSAY #7

Peace of Mind

A TRUCE AT HEART

Is peace of mind something that happens to us, or something we create?

Legend has it that a famous entertainer was once asked how he managed to stay so calm and carefree. Smiling, he reached into his pocket, pulled out a thick wad of cash, and said, "This is why." It's a funny story, and probably untrue, but revealing. It reminds us how easily we confuse external ease with inner peace.

Woody Allen once quipped, "Having money is good, if

only for financial reasons." And yet, a person with ten million dollars is no happier than one with nine. Comfort may reduce inconvenience, but it does not guarantee calm.

Peace of mind comes from what happens within us, not from what happens around us. It is shaped by how our inner world interprets events, not by circumstances themselves. The same situation can leave one person agitated and another untroubled, not because the moment is different, but because of the lens through which it is experienced.

This is why peace of mind is, quite literally, peace of the mind. When our inner narrative shifts, inner conflict softens. When interpretation becomes wiser and more grounded, emotional turbulence gives way to steadiness.

In what follows, we'll explore three expressions of a well-framed inner life: patience, faith, and optimism. Not as traits we must force upon ourselves, but as natural outcomes of a mind that has learned how to live more gently, more honestly, and more fully in the present.

PATIENCE

PEACE WITH THE PRESENT

Patience, often described as long-souled, is an inner calm that emerges when we stop resisting the moment we are in. It is not merely the ability to wait.

Much of our frustration comes not from what is happening, but from the silent argument we carry with it: *This shouldn't be taking so long. This isn't how I planned it. I don't deserve to be treated this way.* When the mind insists that reality is unacceptable or unfair, inner turbulence follows in its wake.

Patience begins when that inner argument is reframed. When we allow the present moment to be what it is, without surrendering responsibility or abandoning hope, tension loosens its grip. The spirit steadies, and what once felt agitating becomes manageable.

This is why patience can calm us in the face of a delayed flight, a forgotten errand, or a missed deadline. Nothing external has changed. What has changed is the way the moment is being experienced. The present is no longer treated as an obstacle to endure, but as a reality to meet.

When peace of mind flows from within, serenity is no longer something we chase. It becomes something we carry, rooted in acceptance of now, and a willingness to live fully where we already are.

FAITH

PEACE THROUGH THE UNSEEN

Faith is the inner calm that emerges when the mind releases its insistence on controlling what it cannot see. It is not blind belief, nor the suspension of reason.

Much of our anxiety is born from an exhausting project: attempting to manage outcomes that lie beyond our reach. We ruminate over conversations that haven't happened, agonize over futures we cannot predict, and attempt to secure guarantees life never promised to give. When the mind appoints itself general manager of the universe, serenity of spirit is unobtainable.

Faith begins when that internal burden is laid to rest. Not

by denying uncertainty, but by recognizing its limits. It is the willingness to say: *I do not see the whole picture, and I do not need to.* In that release, composure returns. The soul no longer strains to hold what was never meant to be carried.

This is why faith steadies us when answers do not come, when prayers seem delayed, or when the path ahead remains unclear. The situation hasn't changed. What has changed is our inner stance. Control gives way to trust, and fear loosens its grip.

In this sense, peace of mind is one of faith's bountiful fruits. It grows when the mind stops demanding certainty, and the soul rests in the knowledge that life has depth and direction, even when those contours remain unseen.

OPTIMISM

PEACE WITH THE FUTURE

Optimism is not the certainty that everything will turn out well. It is the inner freedom that emerges when the mind acknowledges the possibility that things may turn out well.

Much of our anxiety about tomorrow is created today. We project ourselves forward, imagine worst-case outcomes, and live emotionally in moments that may never come to pass. The mind rehearses painful scenarios as if suffering requires preparation. But most of what we fear remains hypothetical, and much of what does arrive proves more manageable than we imagined.

Optimism begins when that rehearsal ends. Not because a positive outcome is guaranteed, but because we recognize that worry does not protect us, it depletes us. When the mind releases its grip on imagined outcomes, energy returns to the present, where clarity and equanimity still reside.

This is why optimism can coexist with realism. It does not ignore risk or refuse responsibility. It simply refuses to confuse foresight with fear. By reframing uncertainty as openness rather than danger, the soul regains its footing. Hope becomes possible, not as wishful thinking, but as intelligent optimism: a clear-eyed recognition that the future may hold more good than we are allowing ourselves to imagine.

In this way, optimism completes the movement of peace of mind. The present no longer feels oppressive, the unseen no longer feels threatening, and the future no longer demands to be solved in advance. Freed from worry, the inner life can rest, rooted in today, open to tomorrow, and confident that whatever comes can be faced when it arrives.

This truth echoes in two very different voices:

> *"A joyful heart is good medicine, but a crushed spirit dries up the bones."*
>
> —PROVERBS 17:22

> *"For peace of mind, we need to resign as general manager of the universe."*
>
> —LARRY EISENBERG, ENGINEER AND WRITER

A QUESTION TO CARRY WITH YOU

When was the last time you felt genuine peace of mind, and what helped you let it in?

Peace returns when we stop wrestling with reality and begin meeting it with wisdom. That question matters, because peace is rarely something we achieve once and for all. More often, it returns in moments, when we stop struggling with reality and allow the inner life to settle into steadiness.

And perhaps that is why peace of mind is not merely a feeling, but a way of seeing.

Peace of mind is not a gift reserved for the lucky. It is a way of living, and a way of seeing. It grows when we stop battling the present, stop demanding certainty from what we cannot control, and stop suffering tomorrow in advance. With patience, faith, and optimism, the inner life becomes steadier, softer, and more free. And even when life remains noisy, the soul can still find its truce at heart

ESSAY #8

Hope

THE COURAGE TO BUILD THE FUTURE

Peace of mind is often the first and necessary response to life's most challenging moments. Like a patient brought into an emergency room, the immediate goal is stabilization: to quiet panic, restore balance, and make space to breathe again.

But stabilization is not the end of healing.

Once the crisis passes, the work shifts from acceptance to rebuilding. Muscles must be strengthened. Movement must return. This second phase requires more than calm. It requires hope.

A man condemned by the king was granted a year's reprieve after assuring his majesty that he could teach the royal horse to fly. If he failed, he would face punishment at the end of the year.

Asked later why he would make such an impossible promise, the man replied, "Within a year, the king may die. Or I may die. Or the horse may die. And who knows? In a year, maybe the horse will learn to fly."

At first glance, his answer sounds absurd. But it wasn't naïve. It was hopeful.

The man did not merely console himself with possibilities. Day after day, he returned to the stable. He acted, believing that the future was still open. Hope does not deny reality. It insists that reality is unfinished, and then it goes to work.

HOPE MOVES US TOWARD A BETTER FUTURE

THE COURAGE TO BEGIN REBUILDING

Hope begins with a vision of a better outcome, and the willingness to move toward it. Obstacles remain real and losses are not denied, but they lose the power to define the final chapter.

Hope, contrary to wishful thinking, is the soul's refusal to remain still. It does not wait for certainty before acting. It begins to build even while questions remain.

To hope is to believe that things can be made better, and step-by-step, to move forward. It is the parent who keeps showing up for a struggling child, not because success is guaranteed, but because love demands effort. It is the community that rebuilds after loss, choosing renewal over retreat.

Hope comes alive when we move forward and bring

possibility into being. It is proactive. And in that movement, a different tomorrow becomes possible.

HOPE REVEALS SOMETHING ABOUT WHO WE ARE

THE SOUL REFUSES TO GIVE DESPAIR THE FINAL WORD

Our capacity for hope tells us something profound about what it means to be human. A train stops when it runs out of tracks. We can keep going even when all the tracks are gone.

When circumstances offer no clear path forward, something within us still leans ahead, refusing to accept that the journey must end.

That forward-leaning instinct is not accidental. It points to something enduring woven into our inner essence: the soul. Hope arises not because conditions improve, but because who we are does not give up. Even when plans dissolve and explanations fail, the soul continues to insist that possibilities have not been exhausted.

Even in our darkest moments, an inner voice insists, *This is not the end.* It does not offer guarantees or timelines. But it encourages forbearance, calm, and thoughtful action. It is a transcendent spark that refuses to let despair have the final word.

Hope endures because it is rooted deeper than circumstance. It emerges from the part of us that was never meant merely to survive, but to grow, to rebuild, and to move forward, even when the way ahead is uncertain.

HOPE IS LIVED BY BUILDING THE FUTURE

VISION BECOMES REAL THROUGH ACTION

Hope does not end in vision. It asks to be lived.

To hope is not simply to wait for circumstances to change, but to participate in their shaping. We are not meant to drift with the current, but to decide where it flows. Hope calls us to assume responsibility for the future, even when its outcome remains uncertain.

This does not require grand gestures. Hope is often expressed through small, deliberate acts: a conversation begun, an effort renewed, a seed planted without certainty of harvest. Each act of hope declares that the present does not have authority over what may come next.

When we act on the soul's insistence that possibilities remain, we discover a form of moral courage that does not depend on guarantees. Dreams may inspire us, but only action gives them form. Hope becomes real at the moment it moves us from imagining a better future to helping bring it into being.

Hope is not blind confidence. It is disciplined commitment. And through that commitment, we do more than endure life as it is. We help bring into being the life that might yet be.

This truth echoes in two very different voices:

> *"Hope deferred makes the heart sick, but a desire fulfilled is a tree of life."*
>
> —PROVERBS 13:12

"Hope is the thing with feathers
That perches in the soul."

—EMILY DICKINSON

A QUESTION TO CARRY WITH YOU

Was there a recent realization, or moment of inspiration, that moved you toward hope?

That question matters, because hope often arrives quietly. Not as certainty, but as a shift. A small inner turning that reminds us there is still something we can do, and still something worth building.

Sometimes hope shows up in the most unexpected places.

A man once stopped to watch a Little League baseball game and asked a boy sitting in the dugout what the score was.

"Eighteen to nothing," the boy replied. "We're behind."

"I'll bet you're discouraged," the man said.

"Why should I be?" the boy answered. "We haven't even gotten up to bat yet."

The boy was not denying the score. He was recognizing opportunity. As long as the game is still being played, there is still a chance to act, and a future that has not yet been decided.

Hope lives in that space, not in certainty, but in participation. It reminds us that as long as there is something we can still do, the story is not over. And the future is still waiting to be built.

SECTION III

Relationships

A person can be wise, reflective, and sincere, and still struggle to connect.

Because the deepest growth is not only inward. It is relational.

Life brings us into contact with other souls, other minds, other stories, and other wounds.

This section explores what it means to build relationships with more care and more courage.

To listen better. To speak more truthfully. To forgive more generously.

To become someone who brings warmth, steadiness, and trust into the lives of others.

In the end, much of spirituality is simply this: learning how to love well.

ESSAY #9

The Healing Touch of Empathy

FEELING WITH OTHERS, NOT JUST FOR THEM

Feeling with others, not just for them, stirs the soul. Empathy draws us into our shared humanity.

A study on postoperative pain found something remarkable: patients spoken to gently and empathetically by their anesthetist needed half as much pain medication and recovered days sooner than those treated with clinical distance.

In other words, compassion didn't only ease the mind. It helped the body heal.

We often think of empathy as emotional, and therefore optional, something nice but not necessary. Yet empathy touches something deeper. When a person feels seen and held in another's awareness, the nervous system calms, the body softens, and healing accelerates.

Empathy isn't merely a social skill. It is a deep spiritual power: feeling another's pain, bridging the distance between souls, awakening something essential within us. Empathy asks more of us than sympathy ever could, but it also gives more, drawing us into genuine connection with others.

RECOGNIZING OUR ONENESS

EMPATHY ENTERS ANOTHER'S WORLD

Sympathy watches pain from afar. Empathy steps inside it. Sympathy says, "I feel sorry for you." Empathy whispers, "I feel with you."

Empathy is the spiritual art of entering another person's world, not to fix it, not to lecture, and not to rush them forward, but simply to be present. To empathize is to see with their eyes and hear with their heart.

To empathize is to bridge the quiet space between souls, carrying part of another's burden as our own. Empathy begins when we stop seeing others as "other," and remember that we are one.

THE CHALLENGE

EMPATHY REQUIRES EFFORT

Empathy is beautiful, and it is hard.

We greet people with "How are you?" every day, but we rarely want a full or honest answer. We may mean well, but we often hope the response will stay simple: "Fine, thank you."

True empathy requires humility, sensitivity, and courage. We turn away from the broken heart because it is difficult to witness. This spiritual numbness isn't malicious. It is protective. To live with an open heart in a world full of suffering requires a willingness to feel, and the courage to help carry another's burden.

Empathy doesn't mean drowning in another person's pain. It means standing close enough to it that they don't feel alone.

GROWING EMPATHY IN THE SOUL

A SPIRITUAL MUSCLE WE CAN STRENGTHEN

Empathy is an act of the soul, a spiritual muscle we can strengthen. It grows through presence, sincere questions, and small deeds that lighten another's load. Sometimes it is a thoughtful message. Sometimes it is a quiet visit. Sometimes it is staying on the phone a few minutes longer than is convenient.

The soul knows what the mind sometimes forgets: "He ain't heavy, he's my brother."

Sharing in sorrow and rejoicing in another's success each deepen the heart. When empathy is expressed with sincerity, we live with genuine caring for others, near and far, and the soul awakens through connection.

This truth echoes in two very different voices:

> *"Do not oppress a stranger; you know the feelings of a stranger, for you were strangers in the land of Egypt."*
>
> —EXODUS 23:9

> *"You never really understand a person until you climb into his skin and walk around in it."*
>
> —ATTICUS FINCH, *TO KILL A MOCKINGBIRD*

A QUESTION TO CARRY WITH YOU

Can you recall a moment when someone didn't just sympathize with you, but felt what you were going through?

That question matters, because the moments we remember most are rarely the ones when someone gave advice. They are the moments when someone entered our experience, and helped us feel less alone.

Empathy transcends sympathy. It is the soul's recognition that another person's burden is our burden, as well. In sharing sorrow and joy, we discover what empathy makes possible: a deeper capacity to feel with others, and a life made more human through connection.

May you be blessed with people who understand you, and may you become that blessing for others.

ESSAY #10

Love and Giving

LOVE GROWS THROUGH RECOGNITION, UNDERSTANDING, AND GENEROSITY

Can you define love? We know it when we feel it, but what makes it grow?

"Oh, 'tis love, 'tis love that makes the world go round," wrote Lewis Carroll in *Alice's Adventures in Wonderland.* Love animates life itself. It is one of the soul's deepest pleasures, and one of the great forces that moves us beyond mere existence into truly living.

This essay explores love not only as something we feel, but

as something we can grow: formed through recognition, deepened through understanding, and strengthened through giving.

LOVE IS A DEEP PLEASURE OF THE SOUL

THE JOY THAT MAKES LIFE FEEL ALIVE

Love is one of life's greatest joys, celebrated in countless songs and stories. It is powerful enough to inspire sacrifice, devotion, and life-changing choices. We crave it because the soul recognizes love as a profound and enduring pleasure.

Animals love instinctively, fiercely protecting their young. Human love, however, widens beyond instinct and kinship, reaching even those we do not know, and ultimately toward something greater than ourselves.

We are drawn to love because we recognize goodness in another: their kindness, strength, sincerity, or wisdom.

That recognition awakens something deep within us. It is as if the soul says: *This is real. This is worth cherishing.*

LOVE GROWS WITH CLARITY AND APPRECIATION

ATTENTION DEEPENS WHAT THE HEART ALREADY FEELS

Most people can sense love, but struggle to define it. Love is an emotion awakened when we recognize the good qualities and virtues of another person, and it grows as deeper knowledge allows us to see those qualities more clearly.

We can't love what we don't know. Attention strengthens love.

Sometimes love is present but hidden, as if our glasses were smudged with yogurt. The world looks blurred, and we assume something is wrong with what we're seeing, when the problem is simply the lens. Remove resentment and ingratitude, and love is released into the soul's open air.

As love deepens through understanding, it naturally creates opportunities to give. The more clearly we see the goodness in another, the more naturally we are moved to give.

LOVE IS STRENGTHENED THROUGH GIVING

HOW THE HEART BECOMES LARGER THAN THE SELF

We often assume we give because we love. But just as often, we love because we give. Giving plants the seeds of love in the human soul.

Parents love their children so deeply in part because they give so much, for so long. The countless acts of care, sacrifice, patience, and attention do not merely express love. They shape it.

Infatuation may fade, but love endures. As a country song puts it: "Honey, I don't care, I ain't in love with your hair. And if it all fell out, well, I'd love you anyway." When comfort and self-interest are set aside, love is freed from illusion and allowed to mature.

Giving does more than benefit the one who receives. It transforms the one who gives. When love is expressed through sustained generosity, it deepens, becoming steadier, wiser, and more resilient over time.

This truth echoes in two very different voices:

"A friend loves at all times, and a brother is born for a time of adversity."

—PROVERBS 17:17

"Love is sharing your popcorn."

—CHARLES SCHULZ

QUESTION TO CARRY WITH YOU

Who or what do you feel a deep love for, and why?

Whatever comes to mind, notice it without judgment. The very fact that you can name what you love is already a sign that your heart is alive and open.

True love rarely arrives with fanfare. It is cultivated through noticing more goodness, understanding more deeply, and giving more freely. When love is tended this way, it grows steadier, stronger, and more enduring over time.

May your love grow in depth and clarity, and may it bring blessing to those you cherish most.

ESSAY #11

Friends Lift Our Soul

TRUE FRIENDSHIP DOESN'T ONLY COMFORT US, IT HELPS US GROW

There is a story about a great scholar who became inconsolable after the death of his closest study partner. Friends, concerned for him, brought one brilliant thinker after another to take the partner's place. Each was articulate, insightful, and eager to help. Yet the scholar rejected them all.

When asked why none of these gifted minds could fill the role, he explained simply: "Whenever I shared an idea, he challenged it, showing me where I might be mistaken. These new partners only tell me why I am correct. That is not what I need."

It is a striking insight. We often think friendship is mainly companionship and emotional support. At its best, it certainly includes those things. But the friendships that shape us most deeply do something more, something profoundly spiritual. They do not merely provide comfort. They awaken the soul.

A true friend is not only someone who walks beside us, but someone who helps us grow inwardly, bringing greater clarity, depth, and spiritual vibrancy into our lives.

Seen this way, friendship is more than a social bond. It is a soul connection, one in which two people become catalysts for one another's growth.

FRIENDSHIP NURTURES GROWTH

THE GIFT OF BEING CHALLENGED WITH LOVE

The deepest friendships are growth-oriented. A true friend is invested in who you can become over time. Through that shared commitment, friendship becomes a gentle force for inner development.

In this kind of friendship, the form and nature of conversation matter. There is a difference between an argument and a discussion. An argument is about winning, proving that one person is right and the other wrong. A discussion is about seeking truth, even when it requires letting go of an initial position.

In true friendship, discussions replace arguments because truth matters more than ego.

When two people connect with trust, vulnerability, and accountability, friendship becomes a source of spiritual vitality.

Growth does not come from constant agreement, but from respectful challenge.

A true friend does not simply affirm who you are. They help you become more fully yourself.

FRIENDSHIP REQUIRES COURAGE

PROTECTING THE BOND THROUGH HONESTY AND CARE

Growth requires courage, especially in friendship. Not only the courage to remain present when things are uncomfortable, but the courage to speak and act when discomfort arises.

A true friend does not want to see a friend harmed, even when that harm is unfolding quietly. Imagine someone drifting in a canoe, unaware that the river ahead drops sharply into a waterfall. Many people might wave from the shore or call out politely. A real friend jumps in, grabs the canoe, and pulls it to safety, even if the friend resists.

FRIENDSHIP TAKES WORK

FRIENDSHIP ISN'T ALWAYS EASY

Similar courage is required in everyday relationships. When small irritations go unspoken because addressing them feels awkward, they accumulate. It's like sweeping dirt under a carpet: eventually, the carpet becomes lumpy. Closeness erodes not because of conflict, but because of avoidance.

Courage in friendship means being willing to raise a significant concern with tact and care. Sometimes there is an explanation. Sometimes there is an apology, even an imperfect one, that relieves a strain and allows the relationship to breathe again.

This kind of courage protects the love and vibrancy of a relationship. When exercised with humility and care, it allows souls to connect more deeply, enabling both people to grow closer, more honest, and more alive.

FRIENDSHIP EMERGES THROUGH GIVING

TO HAVE A FRIEND, BE A FRIEND

The word *friend* is used loosely today. We may call someone we met yesterday "my friend," or accumulate hundreds of so-called friends through social media. But casual connectivity has blurred an essential truth: real friendship cannot be easily acquired.

There is no FriendsAreUs.com. To have a friend, one must first be a friend.

True friendship is formed through effort, giving, and sometimes sacrifice.

A legendary story from the time of the Roman Empire captures this idea. Two lifelong friends lived under different empires. When one was falsely accused in Rome and sentenced to death, he asked to return home briefly to settle his affairs. As a guarantee of his return, his friend agreed to take his place in prison, willing to face execution if he failed to come back.

When the deadline arrived, the accused man returned, and each insisted that the other should live, and that he himself should die. Moved by their loyalty, the emperor spared them both, saying, "I will release you on one condition, that you make me your third friend."

This story points to a deeper truth. Friendship, at its highest level, involves a willingness to bear cost for another, not because it is required, but because bonded friendship demands committed effort.

Yet sacrifice does not usually appear in such dramatic form. A real friend is also someone who gives their time, their energy, and their presence. If you know even one person who, if you called at three in the morning and said, "Please come over, I need your help," would arrive without hesitation or conditions, you are truly blessed.

Someone who has even one such friend is spiritually wealthy. And the path to that wealth is not found in searching for friends, but in becoming one, through consistency, generosity, and the readiness to give of oneself when it truly matters.

This truth echoes in two very different voices:

"... you shall love your friend as yourself ... "

—LEVITICUS 19:18

"A true friend is someone who thinks you're a good egg even though they know you're slightly cracked."

—BERNARD MELTZER

QUESTION TO CARRY WITH YOU

When has a friend's presence lifted your soul in a way you'll never forget? What did they say or do that stayed with you?

Whatever comes to mind, hold it gently for a moment. Because the friendships we remember most are not defined by entertainment or convenience, but by the way they helped us become more alive.

A true friend challenges us without shaming us, protects us without controlling us, and gives without keeping score.

Let's remember: every true friendship, when rooted in growth, courage, and giving, carries sparks of the soul and creates connections that uplift our spirit.

May you be blessed with friendships that lift your soul, and may you lift others in return.

ESSAY #12

The Gift of Forgiveness

FREEDOM BEGINS WHEN WE FORGIVE

There is a story told of a person renowned for exceptional piety. One night, a thief broke into his modest home and fled with a valuable object. Instead of raising an alarm, the man ran after the thief, calling out, "It's yours! I forgive you!"

Stories like this astound us because they stretch our imagination. They describe a moral world larger than our own, one governed not by instinct or self-protection, but by spiritual grandeur. Forgiveness, in such moments, is not weakness. It is a form of transcendence, the capacity to rise above hurt and respond from the deepest part of the soul.

Forgiveness may be one of the hardest gifts to give, yet it can reopen what pain closes. We know the struggle well. We understand that forgiveness matters, and yet resistance often rises within us.

Still, forgiveness is not surrender. It is a profound act of moral and spiritual courage, one that allows relationships, and the human spirit, to breathe again. And because so much of a meaningful life is shaped through relationships, forgiveness becomes one of the great pathways to inner freedom.

FORGIVENESS REOPENS RELATIONSHIPS

RELEASING THE BOND FROM THE GRIP OF THE PAST

Forgiveness can reopen a relationship, even when the other person has not asked for it. When resentment hardens, relationships become guarded and brittle, defined by distance and caution. Forgiveness loosens that grip, creating space for something new to emerge.

Forgiveness does not erase what happened, nor does it excuse harm. What it does is release a relationship from being permanently defined by an experience of discord. Sometimes forgiveness allows closeness to return. Sometimes it allows for honest distance. Either way, it frees relationships from being frozen in the past.

In this sense, forgiveness becomes a gift we give not only to ourselves, but to the relationship itself, allowing it, where possible, to begin again.

FORGIVENESS IS RESTRAINT, NOT SURRENDER

STRENGTH THAT REFUSES TO BECOME BITTER

Forgiveness is restraint, not surrender.

It is the decision to remain governed by our better selves rather than by the injury. It appears as the capacity to hold back when retaliation would feel justified. Ancient wisdom praises those who can absorb an insult without returning it, because they possess the moral clarity and fortitude to preserve dignity and relationship.

There is a story of a man who was once insulted publicly when someone threw a rotten orange at him. Instead of responding with anger, he thanked the offender and said, "I'm grateful you didn't throw a stone."

Forgiveness draws on this same discipline. It resists the initial impulse of retaliation in favor of something more difficult, yet more enduring: the possibility of repair.

This orientation does not mean allowing mistreatment or remaining silent in the face of injustice. Forgiveness can coexist with truth, boundaries, and accountability. What distinguishes forgiveness is not passivity, but the deliberate choice to direct one's response toward healing rather than harm.

When forgiveness is chosen, relationships gain a chance to survive hurt without being consumed by it. That choice reflects not weakness, but moral and spiritual strength, the transcendent capacity to remain human, even when wounded.

FORGIVENESS IS A JOURNEY

THE SLOW WORK OF THE SOUL

Forgiveness often unfolds gradually. Old memories return. Hurt resurfaces. Trust in relationships rebuilds slowly. And forgiveness, like a jigsaw puzzle that takes shape piece by piece, is a process that may take months, or even years.

Forgiveness as a journey acknowledges the complexity of human relationships. Emotional pain does not disappear simply because we decide to forgive. Trust may need rebuilding. Distance may still be necessary.

One way forgiveness grows is through memory, not of what was done to us, but of the times we ourselves have been forgiven. Remembering our own imperfections makes room for humility, and humility creates space for forgiveness. Another way forgiveness is nurtured is through imagination: envisioning what a restored relationship might look like.

Forgiveness does not ask us to expose ourselves again to pain or harm. It does not even mean that reconciliation must occur. Sometimes the most honest form of forgiveness is release, choosing not to carry bitterness forward, even if closeness cannot be renewed.

Seen this way, forgiveness is an ongoing discipline of the soul. It is the inner work of choosing to rise above the hurt, listening to the soul that whispers, "*Take the high road, and do your best to let go.*"

Over time, this practice may change the shape of relationships. Some bonds are repaired. Others are clarified. But in either case, forgiveness allows life to move forward without being burdened by what happened and cannot be undone.

This truth echoes in two very different voices:

"You shall not hate your brother in your heart . . . you shall not bear a grudge."

—LEVITICUS 19:17–18

"An eye for an eye only ends up making the whole world blind."

—MAHATMA GANDHI

A QUESTION TO CARRY WITH YOU

Who in your life might you attempt to forgive, or ask forgiveness from, as a step toward greater peace?

Whatever comes to mind, notice it gently. Forgiveness is not always a dramatic decision. Sometimes it begins as a simple willingness to soften, to take one small step, and to let the soul lead.

Forgiveness rarely happens in one sweeping moment. It is a point and a process, unfolding little by little as we choose peace over bitterness. With each step, relationships gain room to breathe again, sometimes repaired, sometimes gently released, but no longer frozen in pain.

As forgiveness takes root, the soul becomes lighter and freer, and life, in its mysterious way, often invites reconciliation where we least expect it. In choosing forgiveness, we do more than let go of the past. We help shape a future in which connection, dignity, and peace remain possible.

And because relationships are among life's greatest sources of meaning and strength, forgiveness may be one of the most life-giving gifts we ever learn to give.

SECTION IV

Life in the World

The final movement is outward. Not away from the inner life, but through it, and beyond it.

Because what we carry inside us shapes the world we touch.

This section is about living with purpose in the public space of life.

How we view ourselves as part of a greater whole. How we respond to pressure. How we see beauty.

How gratitude becomes action, and how excellence becomes a form of giving.

The goal is not to escape the world, but to bring more light into it, through the life we choose to live.

ESSAY #13

Beauty's Deeper Dimensions

SEEING THE WORLD AS MEANINGFUL

Some things catch the eye. But beauty does more.

We're drawn to it without always knowing why. We sense its presence, yet struggle to define it. Beauty enchants, and at times mesmerizes, stopping us midstep. It can soften us and inspire reverence. It can even bring tears to the eyes.

That tells us something important: beauty is not merely a decoration added to life. It isn't an extravagance reserved for people with refined taste or artistic training.

Beauty seems to bypass the intellect. It is experienced by our inner essence.

That is why beauty has always been connected to spirituality. Not because it is mysterious in a vague or mystical way, but because it touches the soul. It invites us to experience life more deeply. It whispers that the world is not random. It suggests that there is a hidden order beneath what we see, and that we were given the ability to sense it.

Beauty does more than delight us. It calls us upward.

TRUE BEAUTY IS HARMONY

WHEN THE OUTER REFLECTS THE INNER

Beauty isn't only about appearance. It is about alignment. Some kinds of beauty can't be explained, yet their allure is instantly recognizable. Beauty emerges from harmony, when the outside reflects the inside, when what a person shows to the world is not simply an outer garb, but an authentic expression of who they are.

That is why we're drawn to faces that radiate kindness, or to children whose innocence hasn't yet been clouded. Their beauty isn't only in their features. It is in their goodness and purity. We sense we are seeing a soul that has not yet been dulled by moral compromise or cynicism.

And that is why certain people become more beautiful the more we get to know them.

At first, we might notice their smile, their warmth, their grace. But over time, our appreciation deepens. We begin to associate their presence with trust, their steadiness with integrity, and their character with virtue.

Then, almost imperceptibly, they appear more beautiful than they did at first. Why? Because true beauty emanates from the inner core, not merely from what meets the eye.

We do not only see beauty. We recognize it. We feel it. We respond to it.

In the deepest sense, beauty flows from the soul outward. When our outer lives mirror our inner spiritual brilliance, we become not only whole, but luminous.

BEAUTY RESTORES US

GATHERING THE SCATTERED SELF

We are affected by our surroundings more than we realize.

A beautiful home, a peaceful space, or even a small corner of order and tenderness can change our inner world. Beauty captures our attention, gathering our scattered self. In a world that pulls us in multiple directions, beauty has the power to return us to ourselves.

That is why beauty can heal in ways that are subtle, yet real.

Recall a time when you entered a space that felt harsh, chaotic, or neglected. The heart tightened. The nervous system braced. The soul became guarded.

Then remember what occurred when you entered a place that felt gentle, orderly, and touched by grace. The shoulders loosened. The mind settled. Something in us opened.

Not all that glitters is beauty. True beauty softens inner hardness and restores our capacity to feel awe. And once the noise fades, beauty does something even more remarkable: it awakens the soul to notice the sacred moments that move us.

A rising or setting sun.

A melody that carries emotion we didn't know we were holding.

A kind glance from someone who sees us.

A child's laughter, pure and unpretentious.

A face softened by compassion.

Beauty trains the heart to notice what matters. It reminds us that life is not only something to manage. It is something to enter, to feel, and to live more awake.

BEAUTY ELEVATES US

A CUE THAT MEANING IS REAL

Beauty isn't merely for enjoyment. It is a signal.

It is woven into the fabric of existence, reminding us that meaning is real. The design that permeates the universe, from the smallest patterns in nature to the grandeur of the heavens, not only impresses the mind, but informs the soul.

Only human beings can experience beauty as a bridge to spirituality. We can stand before beauty and feel transcendence. We sense that something is being communicated to us. We feel a yearning for what is higher, truer, and more enduring.

True harmony lies where spirit and matter meet. When the physical mirrors the spiritual, beauty becomes more than pleasure. It becomes a path to nobility.

Beauty does something rare: it elevates our desires. It refines our instincts. It stirs our conscience. It urges us to become more than we were yesterday.

Beauty becomes spiritual when it lifts us toward who we

are meant to be: living with refinement, acting with greater dignity, and creating homes and communities that reflect the best of who we are.

In the end, beauty is not only something we admire. It is something that elevates us.

This truth echoes in two very different voices:

> *"Behold, you are beautiful, my beloved; behold, you are lovely … your eyes are like doves."*
>
> —SONG OF SONGS 4:1

> *"Beauty awakens the soul to act."*
>
> —ATTRIBUTED TO DANTE ALIGHIERI

A QUESTION TO CARRY WITH YOU

Beauty wears many faces, some fleeting, some lasting. What moment of beauty has stayed with you, long after it has passed?

Whatever comes to mind, linger there for a moment. Because when we remember beauty, we are not only recalling what we saw. We are remembering who we were in its presence, more open, more awake, more alive.

Beauty is not rare. But our openness to it can be.

When we allow beauty to enter, it restores us, and lifts us toward who we are meant to become.

ESSAY #14

Gratitude: From Heart to Habit

GRATITUDE BECOMES POWERFUL WHEN IT IS LIVED

Gratitude may begin as a feeling, but it becomes meaningful and impactful when it is put into action.

After President John F. Kennedy's assassination, Jacqueline Kennedy received nearly 800,000 messages of condolence. In the months that followed, nearly 900,000 acknowledgment cards were sent on her behalf, ensuring that each expression of sympathy was recognized. The scale is staggering, but what it reveals is even more striking: gratitude can become a steady discipline, even in the shadow of heartbreak.

A smaller story makes the same point in a more ordinary key. In the 1990s, Cathy Keating, the First Lady of Oklahoma, organized a statewide "housewarming" for the governor's mansion. About 1,500 citizens contributed household items and historical furnishings. Over the course of three months, she wrote a handwritten thank-you note to every donor.

When asked why she didn't send a generic message, she explained that she wanted each person to feel the significance of their contribution. She even tailored her notes to the recipient: one tone for a second-grade class, another for the widow of a prominent entrepreneur. How did she manage it?

She wrote whenever she could, in the car, late at night, and on her only day off.

Most of us will never face 800,000 letters, and few of us will ever write 1,500 handwritten notes. But we are presented with the same choice: will gratitude remain a passing emotion, or will it become a way of living?

Gratitude takes many forms. In the ideas that follow, we'll explore three essential truths that can help us grow it from heart to habit, until it becomes not only a private feeling, but a public blessing.

WHAT GRATITUDE LOOKS LIKE

RECOGNITION EXPRESSED OUTWARD

Gratitude shows up in countless ways, sometimes playful, sometimes profound. A little boy once wrote that he was thankful for his eyeglasses, explaining that they kept the boys from hitting him and the girls from kissing him.

It can also be expressed on a grand scale. Richard Chaifetz, who once pleaded for help to stay in college, later donated $12 million to St. Louis University in thanks.

But gratitude isn't measured only by the size of the gesture. It's measured by the depth of recognition.

Classic wisdom teaches that gratitude isn't about having more. It's about taking pleasure in what you already have. That can mean noticing the gifts we often overlook: the ability to see, to walk, to breathe without effort, to taste food, to sleep in safety.

It can also mean appreciating the people we sometimes take for granted, the ones we love, and who love us: listening patiently, sharing burdens, and making life lighter simply by being present.

In other words, gratitude isn't only a response to extraordinary blessings. It is the ability to recognize what is already precious.

And when that recognition is expressed, gratitude becomes more than a feeling. It becomes a way of bringing goodness into the lives of others.

WHAT BLOCKS US FROM GRATITUDE

THE "MORE" TRAP, AND ITS COST

If gratitude is so nourishing, why is it so often overlooked?

One reason is simple: we chase "more." We look at our neighbor's lawn and assume the grass is greener, that a little more money, a little more comfort, a little more recognition will finally satisfy us. Yet many people have had wealth, fame, power, and pleasure, and still died miserable.

Billionaire J. Paul Getty was once asked how much was enough. His answer was chilling in its honesty: "A little bit more."

That single sentence exposes the trap. The myth that things make us happy blinds us to blessings already present. When we live that way, we don't practice gratitude, and we lose joy. We become experts at noticing what we lack, and amateurs at appreciating what we have. There is another misconception that drains gratitude as well: the belief that our unhappiness is our own private business. It isn't. Like a pothole in the road, a sour disposition becomes a public menace. It affects spouses, children, friends, coworkers, and anyone who happens to be nearby.

Gratitude doesn't deny life's burdens, and it doesn't pretend everything is perfect. But it restores perspective. It renews the spirit. And it helps us return to a truth we easily forget: there is far more good in our lives than we regularly acknowledge.

CULTIVATING GRATITUDE

TURNING APPRECIATION INTO CONTRIBUTION

Gratitude is a quality of the soul, and like any spiritual quality, it deepens through deliberate practice. One of the simplest habits is to begin the day by counting blessings, not vaguely, but specifically. You might say to yourself: "I woke up this morning. I can see. I have love in my life." Gratitude is a spiritual muscle, and the more we exercise it, the stronger it becomes.

Another practice is to build "monuments" of remembrance, small reminders that keep us from forgetting. The town of Enterprise, Alabama, did something extraordinary: it erected a monument honoring the boll weevil, the pest that once devastated its cotton crops. Why honor a plague? Because it forced the town to diversify, adapt, and ultimately prosper. Their monument is a reminder that even hardships can contain hidden gifts.

And gratitude should never remain locked inside the heart. Don't let favors go unacknowledged. Thank the person who prepared your meal, taught your children, offered you guidance, or simply held the door. These moments may seem small, but they are the building blocks of a grateful life.

When we live with awareness of our blessings, gratitude transforms our perspective. It softens what is harsh, brightens what is good, and reconnects us to the source of all life. Gratitude is not only an emotion. It is the soul expressing itself, saying, "Life itself is a gift!"

Gratitude changes the atmosphere around us. It makes us more generous, more patient, and more enjoyable to live with. A grateful person doesn't only feel better inside; they become a blessing to the world outside.

This truth echoes in two very different voices:

> *"A joyful heart is good medicine, but a crushed spirit dries up the bones."*
>
> —PROVERBS 17:22

> *"The hardest arithmetic to master is that which enables us to count our blessings."*
>
> —ERIC HOFFER

A QUESTION TO CARRY WITH YOU

What is the one thing you can pause right now to truly savor and appreciate?

Whatever comes to mind, stay with it for a few seconds longer than usual. Because gratitude grows when we stop rushing past the good, and let ourselves feel it fully.

Global happiness surveys often find that some of the happiest people live in countries that are far less wealthy than ours, reminding us that happiness isn't something you can purchase. Across the world, the pursuit of comfort and convenience can make us think that happiness is something we obtain by acquiring more. But that belief overlooks a deeper truth: fulfillment lies not in accumulation, but in appreciation.

Yet there is another way to become rich. We can become happiness billionaires, not by collecting more, but by cultivating gratitude. When we learn to count our blessings, we begin to discover that we have been surrounded by gifts all along.

And when gratitude becomes a habit, it doesn't only change our inner world. It changes the world around us.

ESSAY #15

Becoming Excellent, Becoming You

IT'S A SOUL THING—A LIFE LIVED AWAKE

The name Stradivarius is synonymous with excellence. Antonius Stradivarius refused to release a violin from his workshop until it was as close to perfection as skill and human care could make it. His philosophy was summed up in a single line:

"Other men will make other violins, but no man shall make a better one."

What makes that line so striking is not only its confidence, but its devotion. Stradivarius wasn't merely building instruments. He was shaping something meant to outlast him. His work carried a message that rises from the deepest part of the soul: what you touch matters, and how you touch it matters.

Excellence is not only how we grow. It is how we give.

But is excellence reserved only for rare geniuses like Stradivarius?

Most people assume it is. They hear the word *excellence* and think of extraordinary talent, elite achievement, or people born with gifts they don't possess. They assume excellence belongs to a small category of exceptional human beings, while the rest of us should settle for "good enough."

Yet excellence is not a function of innate genius, or even talent. It is about actualizing what we have been given, and refusing to treat our own potential casually. It is the decision to live with intention, to show up fully, and to do what we do with care.

The question is not whether we can be Stradivarius. The question is whether we are willing to become our fully excellent selves.

To understand excellence more deeply, we need to look beneath the surface.

WHAT IS EXCELLENCE?

THE SOUL EXPRESSING ITSELF THROUGH OUR WORK

Excellence is not an achievement we stumble into. It is the conscious expression of our essential self.

Deep down, we want our lives to matter. We want to fulfill our purpose. We want to leave behind more than memories of busyness. We want to leave a trace of light where we pass.

That longing is not arrogance. It is not ego. It is not perfectionism. It is something deeper: the inner awareness that we were not placed in this world merely to drift through it. Excellence is native to the soul, a drive embedded in our spiritual essence. Settling for mediocrity is counter to our inner nature.

And that is why excellence should not be confused with success.

Success measures how we compare to others. It is often external: titles, applause, awards, status.

Excellence is different. Excellence measures how faithfully we develop what we were given, and how fully we bring it into the world. It is a uniquely personal inner quality, yet it expresses itself outwardly in the way we work, build, serve, create, and contribute.

A person can be successful and still feel hollow. And a person can be excellent in a way the world never applauds, yet their life and work elevate those around them.

Excellence emerges when we orient ourselves to giving our best, and let the soul shape what our hands bring into the world.

THE OBSTACLE TO EXCELLENCE

THE BELIEFS THAT SHRINK US

The greatest impediment to excellence is rarely failure. It is what we believe about ourselves.

When people believe they have potential, they rise to meet it. When they doubt themselves, invisible ceilings take shape. Not because the ceilings are real, but because the mind treats them as real. Over time, those beliefs shape our choices, our habits, and even our identity.

We tell ourselves stories:

"I'm not so creative."

"I don't have a head for numbers."

"I'm not disciplined."

"I'm not the kind of person who follows through."

"Excellence isn't for people like me."

These beliefs become self-fulfilling prophecies. They don't merely describe us. They limit us. And they train us to accept a smaller version of our own life.

Sometimes the obstacle is fear: *What if I try and fail?*

Sometimes it is pride: *What if I try and people judge me?*

Sometimes it is exhaustion: *I don't have it in me.*

And sometimes it is comfort: *I'm fine the way I am.*

But here is the deeper truth: When we lose sight of who we truly are, we don't only diminish our own lives. We also diminish what we bring into the world. We offer less care, less effort, and less contribution, and we accept less than we are capable of achieving.

And that is how mediocrity becomes normal.

Excellence begins when we refuse to accept mediocrity, and remember that the soul was not designed to live small.

ACTUALIZING YOUR EXCELLENCE

TURNING INNER GIFTS INTO OUTWARD IMPACT

Excellence begins when we realign how we see ourselves.

People are created equal, but each of us has a unique combination of strengths, sensitivities, and experiences. Excellence is not about becoming someone else. It is about actualizing the potential within us.

When we stop viewing ourselves as ordinary, something awakens inside us. We remember that our soul is lofty, and our lives are not accidental. We were each given something to develop, something to carry, something to bring into the world. Once that inner shift takes root, a practical path forward becomes clear.

We begin by identifying what truly stirs us, that intersection of curiosity, delight, and purpose. We ask: "*What am I here to build? What am I here to repair? What am I here to give?*"

Then we choose one actionable step.

Excellence requires reaching beyond our zone of comfort. Most breakthroughs don't come from new techniques, but from uncommon depth. What separates adequacy from excellence is rarely genius. It is how fully we show up.

Slowly, we build daily habits that create the extraordinary. Excellence is not a dramatic leap. It is a steady ascent, shaped one faithful step at a time, guided by the soul.

The world has an abundance of those seeking attention. It needs more people bringing their best. Excellence is how we turn our gifts into impact, and our inner light into something others can feel and see.

This truth echoes in two very different voices:

> *"If you are not a better person tomorrow than you are today, what need have you for a tomorrow?"*
>
> —RABBI NACHMAN OF BRESLOV

> *"Bob Gibson is the luckiest pitcher I ever saw. He always pitches when the other team doesn't score any runs."*
>
> —TIM MCCARVER (SAID WITH A WINK)

A QUESTION TO CARRY WITH YOU

Where in your life might you feel invited to become more fully yourself?

Whatever comes to mind, notice it without pressure. Excellence does not begin with grand gestures. It begins with one honest step, taken with intention.

Excellence doesn't ask us to become someone else. Nor is it result-dependent or defined by success. It asks us to become more fully who we already are, with faithfulness, intention, and care.

When we create excellence, we refine ourselves, and we strengthen what we bring into the world. And in doing so, we may leave behind more than accomplishment. We may leave a trace of light.

ESSAY #16

Becoming a Light to Others

ILLUMINATION REVEALS CLARITY AND BEAUTY

The world is full of stories of people who were fired, only later to flourish. Mozart was dismissed from the court of the prince-archbishop of Salzburg. Oprah Winfrey lost her job as a news reporter because her producer thought she wasn't a good fit. Walt Disney was fired by a newspaper editor who claimed he "lacked imagination and had no good ideas."

In hindsight, such moments feel almost laughable. But at the time, they were experienced as failures and darkness. And that is what makes them worth noticing. Because what changed wasn't only their careers. It was the lens through which their lives were eventually understood.

Light does not erase reality. It doesn't rearrange the furniture of our lives or remove every obstacle from the path. But it does something just as powerful: it reveals what is already there. It helps us see meaning where we once saw only loss, direction where we once saw only confusion, and possibility where we once saw only limitation.

Most of us will never be fired and later become household names. But we face our own forms of darkness all the time: a disappointment that stings, a setback that rattles our confidence, a door that closes without explanation. In those moments, the question is not only what happened, but how we will see it.

And this is where light becomes more than comfort. When our soul sees clearly, we don't only feel stronger inside.

We become more capable of bringing illumination into the world around us. We respond with greater wisdom, greater compassion, and greater purpose.

In the ideas that follow, we'll explore three essential truths that can help us see life, and live it, with clarity and meaning.

LIGHT AWAKENS AWARENESS

SEEING WHAT WAS ALWAYS THERE.

Some may assume that light changes the world, but what it changes is our perception. Light doesn't change reality. It reveals it. The room is the same whether the lamp is on or off. What shifts is what we notice, what we understand, and how we respond.

This is one of life's key spiritual insights: the outer world can remain exactly the same, while our inner world shifts dramatically. A person can live with eyes wide open and still miss what truly matters.

Light, in the form of awareness, enables us to notice a loved one's presence instead of taking it for granted. We recognize deeper meaning in a conversation we once dismissed. We see an opportunity within a challenge, rather than only an obstacle.

And this is where light becomes more than personal insight. When our soul sees clearly, we engage with the world differently. We speak with more patience. We judge others with more compassion.

We act with greater wisdom. In a world where confusion often comes from people reacting without perspective, even a little more light can bring remarkable lucidity.

A SMALL LIGHT CAN CARRY ENORMOUS POWER

ONE SPARK CAN CHANGE EVERYTHING

Darkness often feels overwhelming, yet it is easily dispelled. A single flame can change an entire room. Light doesn't need to be large to be real. It only needs to be present.

In difficult moments, the mind tends to speak in absolutes: *This will never get better. I'll never recover. Nothing will change.* But even then, a spark often appears. Sometimes it's a friend's kindness. Sometimes it's a new idea. Other times it's a small act of courage, barely visible, but real. And once that spark appears, it challenges the lie that everything is hopeless.

There is a famous example of this kind of resilience. During a concert, violinist Itzhak Perlman snapped a string. He paused, gathered himself, and finished the piece on three strings. He didn't pretend the loss didn't happen. He didn't demand perfect conditions. He created something beautiful from what remained.

Life can break a "string" in any number of ways: a setback, a diagnosis, a disappointment, a relationship that changes. The question is not whether we feel the loss. The question is whether we decide that the music is over.

Sometimes the most luminous response to darkness is not a dramatic turnaround, but a decision: *I will use what I still have.*

And when we learn that a small light can still shine, we stop waiting for perfect conditions before we act. We become empowered to bring hope, clarity, and strength to others.

BECOMING A LAMPLIGHTER TO OTHERS

SHARING LIGHT UNTIL IT MULTIPLIES

Light is one of the few gifts that becomes stronger when it is shared. It isn't diminished by being given away. On the contrary, it multiplies.

Once we begin to see life with greater clarity, and once we learn that even a small light can stand up to darkness, the next step follows naturally: we were meant to share our light outwardly.

Sometimes that means offering encouragement to someone who feels dim inside. Sometimes it means listening without rushing to fix. Sometimes it means bringing calm into a tense moment.

There is an old image of a person walking through a dark

street with a flame in hand, lighting one lamp after another. He doesn't deny the darkness. He doesn't complain about how much is broken. He simply brings light, one place at a time, until the street begins to change.

And here is the most beautiful truth: the greatest light we can bring to others is helping them discover their own.

Not rescuing them, but strengthening them. Not impressing them, but inspiring them.

Because when one light awakens another, something extraordinary happens. Darkness doesn't temporarily retreat. It loses its power. And the world becomes brighter, not because one person became a spotlight, but because many people were inspired to shine.

This truth echoes in two very different voices:

> *"The entrance of Your words gives light, helping even the simple to understand."*
>
> —PSALM 119:130

> *"Lift me up so I can see*
> *Shine your light on me"*
>
> —THE DOOBIE BROTHERS, *"SHINE YOUR LIGHT"*

A QUESTION TO CARRY WITH YOU

What part of the shaded world might look different if you spread your light there?

Whatever comes to mind, don't overthink it. Light doesn't always arrive through grand gestures. Often it begins with one small act, offered with sincerity.

Some say that sunshine is the best disinfectant. But light does more than cleanse. Light illuminates. It turns confusion into clarity, fear into courage, and isolation into connection.

Each of us is given a measure of light, not only to see our own path, but to help others find theirs. And when we choose to share it, we become part of something larger: a chain of illumination that pushes back the darkness, one lamp at a time.

About the Author

RABBI ZE'EV SMASON is a teacher, writer, and spiritual guide dedicated to making timeless wisdom accessible and meaningful in everyday life.

Drawing on years of study and teaching, his work speaks to readers from all backgrounds, presenting ideas that are both deeply rooted and relevant.

He believes that spirituality is not separate from life, but expressed through how we think, relate, and live each day.

Rabbi Smason lives in St. Louis, Missouri, with his wife, Chani. He enjoys cheering for UCLA sports teams, sharing jokes and puns with his children and grandchildren, and exploring biographies and linguistics.

He also writes a weekly newsletter, *Spiritual Sparks*, offering reflections on living with greater purpose, awareness, and connection. To subscribe, visit spiritualsparks.beehiiv.com/subscribe

www.ingramcontent.com/pod-product-compliance
Lightning Source LLC
LaVergne TN
LVHW090531110826
845146LV00003B/1060